songs of snow
and silence

songs of snow and silence

WORDS BY **JEN EMERY**

PAINTINGS BY **LORETO RUIZ**

atmosphere press

For Jimena, Tommy, Barbara, Frankie, Esther and Gabriel.
Whisper your desires and walk them home.

In the 17th and 18th centuries, Stradivarius created some of the finest violins ever made. As they age, they will soon become too fragile to play, and their unique sound risks being lost. In 2019, the Museo del Violino in Cremona embarked on a project to record the sounds of the violins for posterity.

Imagine, first, a forest full of snow —
this is long ago and far away.
Imagine day, the low sun slanting
through trees. Imagine it has been this way
forever; yet still the old and mad believe
that times will change and silence break
and all the trees stir from their quiet vigil
to sing, touched by a gentle breeze.

Imagine this place cracked by a violent shout.

Gloved hands clapping, hot plumes of breath.

Men, horses, a sleigh, a glinting axe,

the crunch and snap of a blade on wood, and then —

the green smell of a new wood-wound,

the sky broken open.

A woodlark tumbles, spirals high, piercing
the startled air with his crystal cry.

Now, travel west, and perhaps some years roll by us,
and come to Cremona, to a townhouse in a square.
Late evening, early spring in 1654 –
the windows thrown wide to catch the softest whisper
of warmth in the air. Upstairs around a fireplace,
old friends are singing songs, telling stories
to heal old wounds and right old wrongs. And a little boy
sits quietly listening, wondering where he belongs.

This is Antonio Stradivari,
born on the run in a winter of hunger and fear.
He learned to walk on a long and lonely road,
learned to sing around a fire in the darkness,
his ear tuned to a flickering beauty.
Tonight, his brothers make fine silhouettes
before the fire – tall necks, broad chests
full of songs and echoing with laughter.

But Antonio knows that the fire will flicker and die,
that the beauty in song is the catching of loss in our throats,
an empty belly echoes more than a full one,
a bird disturbed and fleeing sings the purest notes.
And so he's a boy who listens to silence, and seeks
the swift glimpses of joy that dance in the moments beneath –
the drawn breath, the words unsaid,
the way laughter can sound like grief.

At twelve years old, young Nino is apprenticed
to Pescaroli the woodcutter. His days
are long now and heavy with dust and his fingers ache,
but there's something about this intimate craft and the ways
the wood will whisper where to place his mark
to reveal the pattern laid down in the dark
long ago, beneath deep snow
and the cry of a single lark.

One spring, the luthier Amati calls for a craftsman,
so Pescaroli sends the boy to a room hung with violins,
the sun slanting low through the windows,
a space full of silence in which creation begins.

Nino lifts a violin and the emptiest part
of the boy on the lonely road sings: this instrument art
breaks silence to make perfection
and captures his heart.

For years, the boy loiters on workshop thresholds,
runs errands for maple offcuts, buys an old mould,
spends his nights by candlelight, listening
to the songs in the wood, the stories not yet told.

A violin's belly, he learns, is a silent dark –
a heart, a moment in time that holds through years
his brothers' fireplace laughter, a single lark
his mother's face, a manuscript of tears.

Stradivari sells his first violin.

Then another. Dozens. Hundreds. The years roll by.

He falls in love, buys a house, has children.

It looks as though he's made it! But the cry

of a lark above a snow-filled wood still calls;

the slightest shift in breadth, depth, tone enthralls;

and his hands ache to keep breaking the silence,

to create transcendence, to hold it all.

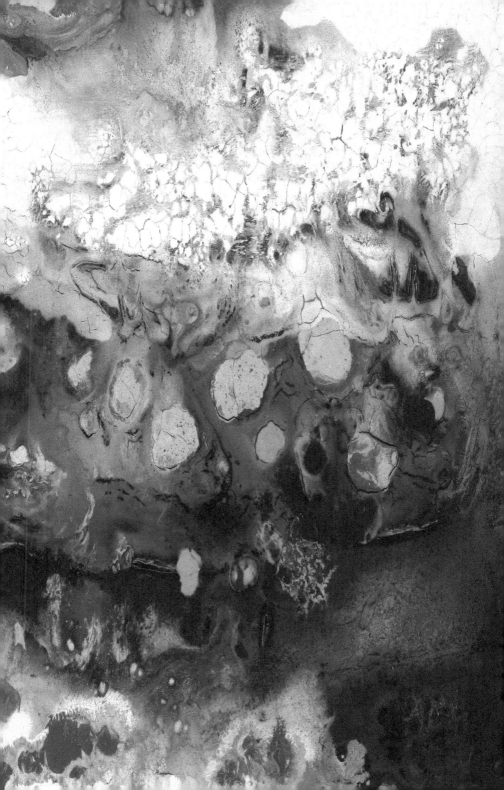

Let's pause here for a moment, simply to gaze
on the beauty born beneath this master's hand –
the quarter-cut maple, the f-holes, scrolls, purfling.
In the exquisite arc of his instruments, we understand
that here is a work for the ages: ancient ratios,
and the science and art of a moment in time enclose
in silence songs sung over centuries –
bright sky, dark forest, deep snow.

When Stradivari is fifty-four,

his reputation made, his children grown,

Francesca, his love of thirty short years, dies

and once more he's on a long road, all alone.

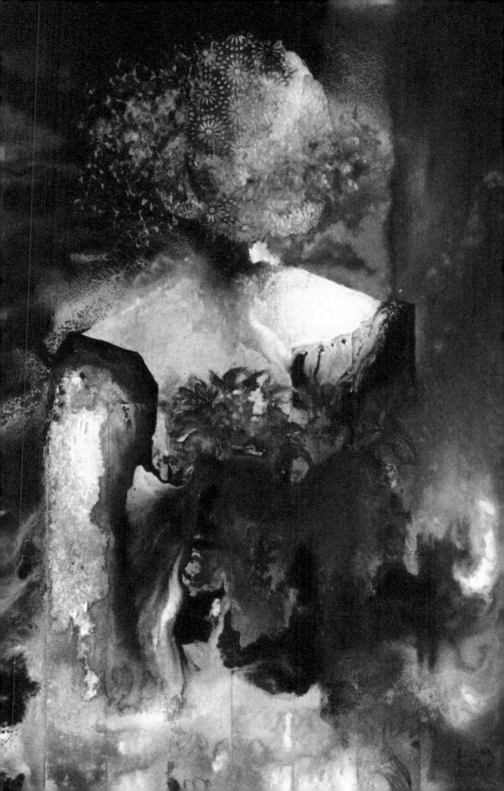

Where to now for this seeking, striving boy?
Broken silence and a broken heart.
The quietest forest calls, but does a lark
yet leap high in a fractured sky – *joy joy joy?*

Have you lived long enough yet to know what it is to wake
stiff and cold before dawn by a burned-down fire?
Half a century told in fragments of old songs,
drifting as embers on the morning air:

love and loss, music and silence, death and birth
float and fall and clothe Nino in their ashes.
He whispers his desire, and walks it home
to the broken place where heaven touches earth –

and reaches the golden age! A workshop full
of industry and sunlight. Maple dust
shadows the master's movements, smooth and swift,
his eyes ablaze, his fingers stained deep rust.

The soundboxes perfect, the edges sure and broad,

the scrolls adorned and far and wide, the word

that an old man in Cremona

possesses the hands of God.

But an instrument lives longer than its craftsman,
can find its voice only after its maker has died.
In 1737, Stradivari is laid to rest,
yet the timeless mysteries he caught inside
his perfect hands will move the hearts of throngs
evoking snow-filled forests, fireside songs
sung long ago by a little boy,
wondering where he belongs.

Those we love, we name, as if to stake a claim —
and so, in time, with Stradivarius violins:
The Red, the Baron Knoop, the Lady Blunt,
the Cipriani Potter, Le Fountaine.

Hundreds of Strads, passed hand to hand down centuries,
played by maestros, stolen, copied, traded
for love, for gold, or just to hold
the weight and space of a violin in its heyday.

What is it in us that longs to possess, to take?
We cannot own a sunrise, hold music, or lock-up love
and so instead those rich enough buy tokens:
a house on a hill facing east, a lover's glove,
a violin low-lit in a glass cabinet
inviting our envy and lust –
birdsong and firesong silenced,
the snow greyed to a blanket of dust.

Did you imagine it would be this way forever?
Or did you know that there would come an hour
when the lark would not sing, the snow melt to spring,
and bring us all, broken, to silence?

Or perhaps you have learned, like Nino, that love outlives us?
That the silence, once broken, will hold forever your song.
Each maker dies, each instrument, but still
the music and the moment will live on.

So come once more to Cremona, in 2019,
on a January morning, to a museum on a square.
The roads around are closed to traffic, residents
mime their coffee orders on the air,
touch cheek to cheek in greeting, commute in plimsoles.
A mother picks up a crying child, consoles
her with smothering kisses, and all around
the city holds its breath.

In the museum, one man with a violin
sits, bow poised, until silence falls like snow,
then begins: flurries of scales and arpeggios
drifting as embers, captured forever, remembered
as songs round a fire long ago. We say 'to give ear to',
and indeed it is a gift; we fall silent
as we would fall in love. And in the quietness,
we in turn are gifted a moment to listen —

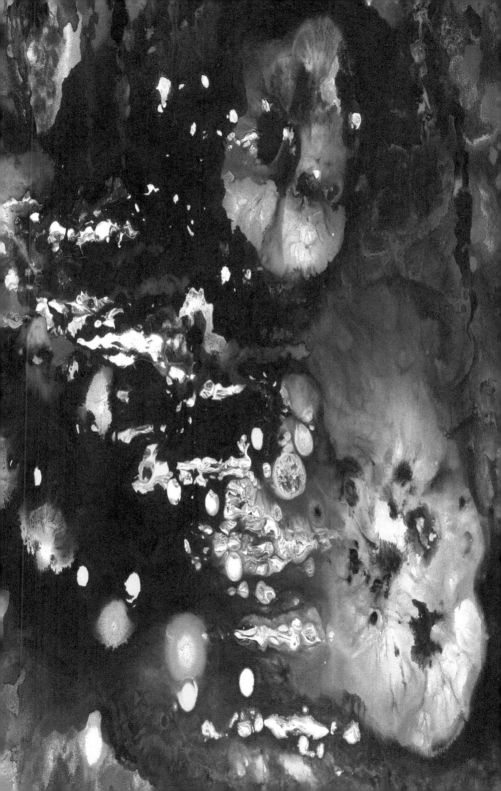

and this alone is enough. We are gifted forever
the promises of a forest full of snow,
the song of a woodlark circling above,
the crack of an axe far below.

We are gifted a joy made only in heartbreak
and music that only our children will know,
all carried to us through centuries
in the hands of the master, Antonio.

painting glossary

"Songs of Snow and Silence"
Somosierra serie. Acrylic and ink on canvas.
120x60 cm.
Pages 2 & 3

Detail of "Songs of Snow and Silence"
Page 5

"To be found… First get lost"
Painting I of a diptych. Acrylic and ink on canvas. 60x90 cm.
Page 6

"Wind Hills"
Triptych. Acrylic and ink on canvas.
30x30-20x30-30x30 cm.
Pages 8, 9, & 33

"Toscana Balcony"
Acrylic and ink on canvas.
50x70 cm.
Page 11

"Cremona I"
Acrylic and ink on board.
50x70 cm.
Pages 12 & 13

"Fire" Light & Shadow serie
Acrylic and ink on canvas.
30x40 cm.
Page 15

"Cremona II"
Acrylic and ink on board.
50x70 cm.
Pages 18 & 19

"Back to my Roots"
Acrylic and ink on canvas.
70x60 cm.
Page 21

"Mediterraneo"
Acrylic and ink on canvas.
100x50 cm.
Pages 22 & 23

"Just Flow" Reflection
serie
Acrylic and ink on
canvas. 100x100 cm.
Pages 24 & 25

"Ice Tales" I &
II Diptych
Acrylic and ink
on canvas. 30x30
cm.
Pages 27 & 38

Detail of "Songs of Snow and Silence"
Page 29

"Fade Away"
Acrylic and ink on canvas.
60x90 cm.
Page 31

"Life Story" Stratos serie
Acrylic and ink on paper. 60x80 cm.
Pages 17, 34 &35, 40 &41

"Desert Rose" Stratos serie
Acrylic and ink on canvas.
80x60 cm.
Pages 36 & 37

Detail of "Donde descansan los recuerdos"
Page 43

"Donde descansan los recuerdos" (where memories rest) Triptych Acrylic and ink on paper. 150x70 cm. Pages 44 & 45

"Cremona III"
Acrylic and ink on board. 50x70 cm.
Page 49

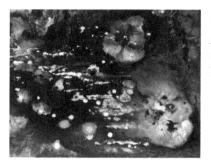

"Passion" Reflection serie
Acrylic and ink on canvas.
90x60 cm.
Page 51

"Mist to Eternity"
Somosierra serie
Acrylic and ink on
canvas. 120x60 cm.
Pages 52 & 53

About Atmosphere Press

Atmosphere Press is an independent, full-service publisher for excellent books in all genres and for all audiences. Learn more about what we do at atmospherepress.com.

We encourage you to check out some of Atmosphere's latest releases, which are available at Amazon.com and via order from your local bookstore:

Damaged, poetry by Crystal Wells

I Would Tell You a Secret, poetry by Hayden Dansky

Aegis of Waves, poetry by Elder Gideon

Footnotes for a New Universe, by Richard A. Jones

Streetscapes, poetry by Martin Jon Porter

Feast, poetry by Alexandra Antonopoulos

River, Run! poetry by Caitlin Jackson

Poems for the Asylum, poetry by Daniel J. Lutz

Licorice, poetry by Liz Bruno

Etching the Ghost, poetry by Cathleen Cohen

Spindrift, poetry by Laurence W. Thomas

A Glorious Poetic Rage, poetry by Elmo Shade

Numbered Like the Psalms, poetry by Catharine Phillips

Verses of Drought, poetry by Gregory Broadbent

Canine in the Promised Land, poetry by Philip J. Kowalski

PushBack, poetry by Richard L. Rose

About the Author

Jen Emery thinks, writes and speaks about work and life in all its messy beauty. Her poetry has been published in magazines including Atrium, Brittle Star and Mslexia, and her business book Leading for Organisational Change was shortlisted for Business Book of the Year in 2019. Jen was born and raised in Edinburgh and now lives in London with her family. You can find her at www.jenemery.com.

About the Artist

Loreto Ruiz is a contemporary artist, architect and designer, who seeks to capture life's most fleeting moments in works that will last forever. Loreto takes her inspiration from nature, leaving space for mystery and the viewer's imagination to complete her work and bring meaning to it. She lives in Madrid with her family. You can find her on Instagram at @ruiz.loreto.

Lightning Source UK Ltd.
Milton Keynes UK
UKHW020246231121
394402UK00006B/684